W9-BFP-486

"An interesting book, lots of tips and techniques for growing food in small spaces."

— Ruby J. Allman, Amazon Reviewer

"If you start out small as a beginner I think this would be the right guide. Good ideas and easy to do."

— Nash, Amazon Reviewer

"Such a cool book and a must have for anyone wanting to grow their own food or make a start at learning how to...whether you want to do it as a hobby or make a serious effort to grow the food you eat this book is a great opportunity to learn how to."

— CLG, Amazon Reviewer

"Loved this book! I am new at gardening and this step by step book will help with the indoor garden I'm planning."

— Daisy, Amazon Reviewer

"This book is wonderful for seniors who like to garden but have restricted mobility."

— Judi A. Smith, Amazon Reviewer

This book is for you if you if you have limited space and want to grow plants of various kinds. Urban Gardening is a very useful introduction to growing a variety of plants in limited space. It is filled with great ideas of how you can get greenery sprouting in your limited space.

— S. Roystone Neverson, Amazon Reviewer

"Great book for those new to gardening... lots of ideas for gardening in limited spaces and seasoned gardeners too."

— bgreg, Amazon Reviewer

URBAN GARDENING

HOW TO GROW FOOD IN ANY CITY APARTMENT OR YARD
NO MATTER HOW SMALL

WILL COOK

All Rights Reserved © Authentic Health Coaching, 2012

Want to connect with like-minded urban gardeners from all over the world? Come join us on Facebook to share your urban gardening questions, ideas, pictures and be a part of the global gardening community!

Join us at http://on.fb.me/HmllNU

TABLE OF CONTENTS

WHY YOU SHOULD READ THIS BOOK 1

INTRODUCTION 4

CHAPTER 1. WHY GROW AN URBAN GARDEN? 5

CHAPTER 2. CHOOSING A SITE FOR YOUR URBAN GARDEN 8

CHAPTER 3. GROWING PLANTS INDOORS 12

CHAPTER 4: DESIGNING YOUR URBAN GARDEN 30

CHAPTER 5: PREPARING THE SOIL FOR YOUR URBAN GARDEN................49

CHAPTER 6: PROPERLY WATERING YOUR URBAN GARDEN 57

CHAPTER 7: HOW TO CHOOSE PLANT CONTAINERS 60

CHAPTER 8: DIY SELF-WATERING PLANT CONTAINERS 65

CHAPTER 9: HOW TO START SEEDS INDOORS...70

CHAPTER 10: CHOOSING PLANTS FOR YOUR URBAN GARDEN.................76

CHAPTER 11: PROTECTING YOUR PLANTS FROM SUMMER AND WINTER.82

CHAPTER 12: COMMON INSECT PROBLEMS IN GARDENS 89

CHAPTER 13: WHAT IS AEROPONICS?..91

CHAPTER 14. ENJOYING YOUR URBAN GARDEN 94

EXCERPT FROM THE CONTAINER GARDENING BOOK 96

ABOUT THE AUTHOR...105

OTHER RECOMMENDED BOOKS ON GARDENING 106

ONE LAST THING... 107

Why You Should Read This Book

I believe every person on this planet deserves access to fresh, local, organic food straight from the farm. The only problem is over 82% of Americans live in a city! So how do you start a farm in an urban environment?

That's why I wrote this book! To show how you or anyone with a little interest in gardening can start a garden in any city, anywhere on this planet and enjoy fresh, organic food, flowers and the fun of gardening.

You could be just months away from a harvest of delicious, fresh organic food from your urban garden!

If you live in a city and have always wanted a garden, this book will help you regardless of your living situation. Whether you have a tiny yard or no yard, a small balcony or no balcony, a rooftop or no rooftop, we'll be tackling all the obstacles that stop most urbanites from growing the garden of their dreams.

There Are No Limitations

No matter where you live on this amazing planet, you too can grow your own fresh food right at home – in any city, anywhere, all year round! Want to grow your own fresh food like this?

All it takes is a little inspiration combined with the information in this book and you can soon be harvesting your own amazing food right at home whether you live in an apartment or only have a tiny 3 ft by 4 ft yard.

The truth is we need people like you – people who care about growing fresh, organic amazing food right at home without relying on big agribusiness. We need to take back control of our food supply and food systems.

TABLE OF CONTENTS

Why You Should Read This Book

Introduction

Chapter 1. Why Grow An Urban Garden?

Chapter 2. Choosing A Site For Your Urban Garden

Chapter 3. Growing Plants Indoors

Chapter 4: Designing Your Urban Garden

Chapter 5: Preparing the Soil for Your Urban Garden

Chapter 6: Properly Watering Your Urban Garden

Chapter 7: How to Choose Plant Containers

Chapter 8: DIY Self-Watering Plant Containers

Chapter 9: Tips for Saving Your Seeds

Chapter 10: Choosing Plants for Your Urban Garden

Chapter 11: Protecting Your Plants from Summer and Winter

Chapter 12: Common Insect Problems in Gardens

Chapter 13: What is Aeroponics?

Chapter 14. Enjoying Your Urban Garden

Excerpt From The Container Gardening Book

About The Author

Other Recommended Books on Gardening

INTRODUCTION

Urban gardening is a term that's been growing in popularity all across the world, especially in developed countries like the United States, Japan, Germany, the United Kingdom and others. The days of needing an acre of land to plant food and herbs are long gone. Today, it's all about gardening in whatever space that you have. So if all you've got is a small backyard or even a patio, putting it to use the best way you know how is all that's needed.

In this book, you will learn about urban gardening methods that can be used for different varieties of properties. As some gardeners say, if you've got a square foot of space, you have enough to grow! In an urban garden, you'll be able to grow pretty much anything that space will allow, including fruits, herbs and vegetables.

After you read this book, hopefully you will take the initiative to join the movement of urban gardening that is spreading rapidly across our wonderful planet!

CHAPTER 1. WHY GROW AN URBAN GARDEN?

Whether you're looking to save money, enjoy picking fresh produce from your own garden or to prepare yourself for an economic or agricultural collapse, urban gardening is an excellent choice. No matter where you live – in a neighborhood or in a condo in the heart of the city – you can enjoy the fruits of urban gardening labor.

Some people have to live in the city although they are country gals or guys at heart. But this shouldn't take you away from your desire to create a beautiful garden! Then there are others who are just learning about gardening but have yet to really delve into it because of limitations of city life.

You may have seen empty spaces in the city being transformed into gardens by community members or even rooftops being made into gorgeous green havens. You too can be a part of urban gardening and it doesn't have to be hard or expensive. I think you'll be surprised at how easy it is. And I know you're going to love your urban garden!

Before you know it, you could have a mini garden that gives you enough ingredients or veggies to last you through the warm months. If you so choose, you can even use growing methods that will allow you to produce food all year long, growing indoors in the winter months if necessary.

Overall, if you live in a building or a house that has a small yard (or no yard!) you don't have to be left out of the world of gardening. You too can save money and enjoy fresh food for you and your family!

GROW YOUR OWN FRESH, LOCAL, ORGANIC AND SAFE FOOD

Every month on the news we hear about a new outbreak of e. coli in spinach or food poisoning or contamination or the dangers of GMO crops...

I believe food should be safe, delicious, healthy and available to everyone! But the only way we're going to get back to a healthy, safe, sustainable food supply is to take back control over our land and grow it ourselves. Just over a hundred years ago, over 90% of Americans lived on farmland. Today, only 2% do!

Over 82% of Americans live in cities! What if we turned our cities back into farmland, growing healthy, delicious, fresh organic food for everyone to enjoy? We can do it with the help of people like you!

GROWING HEALTHIER COMMUNITIES

Urban gardening isn't just a great way to grow fresh, healthy food – it's also a great way to build communities, connect with others and change the world one person at a time. Studies have shown that communities that garden have less crime and residents have less stress and live healthier, longer lives. What if you started a community garden in your city that changed your neighborhood forever, even if you moved away once it started?

What if you could grow a garden that would turn into a legacy and change the lives of future generations? I'm telling you it's possible!

Make Your City More Beautiful

Another huge benefit of urban gardening is that it makes your city more beautiful. Imagine if every abandoned alley and yard in your city was filled with a gorgeous garden, blossoming with ripe tomatoes, watermelons, squash, cucumbers, peppers, kale, bok choy, fennel, dill, lettuce and fresh flowers! Would you feel better about where you live?

Chapter 2. Choosing A Site For Your Urban Garden

The first step to growing is to choose your gardening site. What kind of spaces do you have to work with?

Depending on the type of building you live in and the available space around it, you might be able to grow a lot or a little. You can find space inside of your home and outside. The types of plants you want to grow should also be taken into consideration – some plants grow better outdoors while others flourish inside where they can be nurtured.

Using Your Balcony or Patio for Urban Gardening

If you have a balcony, patio or even a deck outside your home, you can use the outside perimeter (or even the middle space, depending on how often you use it as a sitting space) to build your urban garden. You can use containers to plant your vegetation and hang them on shelves on the walls or place them on the floor in neat rows. To make watering them easier, you can place the containers on top of tables. Some even build a shelf or pole over the railing so that they can hang additional plants.

You can also use your balcony to set up a vertical garden or vertical aeroponics system to grow 20-30 food plants or more in a small space.

PLANTING ON THE ROOFTOP

If allowed, you can use the roof space of your building to grow a garden. Make sure to ask the building's superintendent before pursuing this so that you won't get into trouble!

You can designate a certain amount of square footage to your urban garden. It would be great if you could even use the entire rooftop. Try to get other tenants in the building to join you and enjoy the benefits of the garden. This will even make the work easier since you will have others pitching in to help you.

If your landlord is hesitant about a rooftop garden or says no altogether, you can put together a formal presentation to show how much money will be saved by having a rooftop garden that reduces heating/cooling bills and remediates excess runoff, along with making the roof last longer!

USING YOUR YARD

If you live in a suburb or happen to be one of the few lucky urban dwellers with a yard, of course you can use that space to grow an incredible garden full of fresh food! How big is your yard? If you don't have the measurements, I recommend just taking some quick measurements with measuring tape to get an idea of the area you have to work with.

Also be careful in your planning that you plan enough area for sitting and lounging as well as gardening. I recommend leaving at least a small patch of grass if you can so that you can enjoy the soft grass on your feet and get grounded in the Earth without getting muddy in the soil.

TEAM UP WITH OTHERS TO BUY A PLOT OF LAND

If you have no balcony, yard or usable rooftop, you can buy your own plot of land either by yourself or team up with others in your community!

There's unused space throughout every major city, so see if you can find a plot of land that is just rotting away unused. You've likely seen projects being done in metro areas where a plot of land is cleaned up and transformed into a beautiful plush garden. It's amazing how easy it can be and when everyone is enthusiastic about making it happen, the garden seems to sprout gracefully from all the love. It's also a great project to involve kids in. In order to make this happen, you should either find a plot and go to the City Clerk to find out who owns the property and how you can possibly rent it or purchase it (if you're lucky, it'll be owned by the city). If you can gather enough people, everyone can chip in to pay off the debt.

GROWING INDOORS

The final option for urban gardening is growing indoors. We'll cover that right now in great detail in the next chapter.

CHAPTER 3. GROWING PLANTS INDOORS

Who said that you have to have plants growing outside?

If you don't have the luxury of having a yard, balcony or rooftop for gardening you can grow plants in the comfort of your own home. Just make use of the windowsills throughout your property. You can build shelves for the ones that don't have a sill. Some people even have a vertical garden on their walls, which can be constructed with shelves or pockets on a board. There are different designs available for these – some you can even build yourself. Another great option is to use a vertical aeroponics system near a window to grow 20-30 plants in a 2 ft by 2ft area. More on that in Chapter 13.

If you don't get enough sunlight coming into your home because of your location, you can opt to buy artificial lighting, called grow lights. Make sure to purchase grow lights that are specifically designed for plants. Not just any light bulb can be used. Also, you'll need to have the right temperature and amount of light spectrum (red, white and blue light) for your plants. Some grow better under red light, while others need the full spectrum.

CHOOSING A SITE THAT HAS PLENTY OF LIGHT OR SHADE

When it comes to choosing a site for your plants, it's important that you know all you can about how to nurture and grow them. This means researching whether that specific plant needs majority sunlight or majority shade. You can set up your urban garden in a way that will allow this to work out for each of your plants. For instance, you can have some plants facing south where it will get plenty of light and others in front of larger plants, so that it will get lots of shade. Not paying attention to this important detail could leave you with shriveled, withering plants that are dying from excessive or insufficient sunlight.

If you're planting from seed, the seed packets should tell you how much sun your plants need. Otherwise, just Google it to found out. For example, you can search "Sun Requirement For Tomatoes" to find out how much sun tomato plants need to produce fruit.

CONTAINERS, WALL GARDENS, WINDOW GARDENS AND AEROPONIC SYSTEMS

The easiest ways to garden indoors are to use containers, an aeroponics system, window garden system or a wall garden. We'll cover container gardening and wall gardening in the next chapter. Aeroponics systems are covered in Chapter 13.

Right now let's talk about window gardening.

Above is a picture of a typical "Window Garden" made using plastic bottles. You can either manufacture them yourself or buy a complete system like those found at windowfarms.com

Here's a complete video tutorial for you if you want to grow your own window garden using plastic bottles: http://bit.ly/Tvf0UG

Personally, I don't recommend using plastic bottles for food gardening as the phthalates and other chemicals can leach into the food. I'd much prefer to use food safe plastic to grow to avoid any contamination. But that's just my opinion. If you want to make your own window garden with old plastic bottles, by all means go for it!

Above is a picture of the Windowfarm system which start at $199.

I only recommend window gardening if you just want a few plants or flowers and are looking more for decoration than production. If you're looking to grow enough food to make a sizeable dent in your food budget and eat more fresh food from your own garden, I'd recommend a vertical growing aeroponics system like those found in Chapter 13 because you'll get 8-10 times as much food for about 2-3 times the cost.

LIST OF PLANTS THAT CLEAN THE AIR

The following is a list of amazing plants you can grow indoors that help clean and purify the air you breathe. These plants are perfect for anyone who has allergies or frequent respiratory infections (colds, viruses, flus, etc.). They're also just great for anyone who loves breathing clean air and gorgeous plants!

ALOE (ALOE VERA)

This easy-to-grow, sun-loving succulent helps clear formaldehyde and benzene, which can be a byproduct of chemical-based cleaners, paints and more. Aloe is a smart choice for a sunny kitchen window. Beyond its air-clearing abilities, the gel inside an aloe plant can help heal cuts and burns. You can also make smoothies with the inside flesh of the aloe (just avoid the outer green flesh as it will make you very regular!)

SPIDER PLANT (CHLOROPHYTUM COMOSUM)

Even if you tend to neglect houseplants, you'll have a hard time killing this resilient plant. With lots of rich foliage and tiny white flowers, the spider plant cleans the air of chemicals including benzene, formaldehyde, carbon monoxide and xylene, a solvent used in the leather, rubber and printing industries.

GERBER DAISY (GERBERA JAMESONII)

This bright, flowering plant is effective at removing trichloroethylene, which you may bring home with your dry cleaning. It's also good for filtering out the benzene that comes with inks. Add one to your laundry room or bedroom — presuming you can give it lots of light (south-facing windows are best!).

SNAKE PLANT (SANSEVIERIA TRIFASCIATA 'LAURENTII')

Also known as mother-in-law's tongue, this plant is one of the best for filtering out formaldehyde, which is common in cleaning products, toilet paper, tissues and personal care products. Put one in your bathroom — it'll thrive with low light and steamy humid conditions while helping filter out air pollutants.

GOLDEN POTHOS (SCINDAPSUS AURES)

Another powerful plant for tackling formaldehyde, this fast-growing vine will create a cascade of green from a hanging basket. This is the perfect plant for city dwellers because car pollution is a big concern and car exhaust is filled with formaldehyde. (Bonus: Golden Pothos, also known as devil's ivy, stays green even when kept in the dark.)

Golden Pothos

CHRYSANTHEMUM (CHRYSANTHEIUM MORIFOLIUM)

The colorful flowers of a mum can do a lot more than brighten a home office or living room; the blooms also help filter out benzene, which is commonly found in glue, paint, plastics and detergent. This plant loves bright light, and to encourage buds to open, you'll need to find a spot near an open window with direct sunlight.

Red-edged Dracaena (Dracaena marginata)

The red edges of this easy dracaena bring a pop of color, and the shrub can grow to reach your ceiling. This plant is best for removing xylene, trichloroethylene and formaldehyde, which can be introduced to indoor air through lacquers, varnishes and gasoline.

WEEPING FIG (FICUS BENJAMINA)

A ficus in your living room can help filter out pollutants that typically accompany carpeting and furniture such as formaldehyde, benzene and trichloroethylene. Caring for a ficus can be tricky, but once you get the watering and light conditions right, they will last a long time.

Azalea (Rhododendron simsii)

Bring this beautiful flowering shrub into your home to combat formaldehyde from sources such as plywood or foam insulation. Because azaleas do best in cool areas around 60 to 65 degrees, they're a good option for improving indoor air in your basement if you can find a bright spot.

ENGLISH IVY (HEDERA HELIX)

A study found that the plant reduces airborne fecal-matter particles (who knew that was an issue?!). It has also been shown to filter out formaldehyde found in some household cleaning products.

WARNECK DRACAENA (DRACAENA DEREMENSIS 'WARNECKII')

Combat pollutants associated with varnishes and oils with this dracaena. The Warneckii grows inside easily, even without direct sunlight. With striped leaves forming clusters atop a thin stem, this houseplant can be striking, especially if it reaches its potential height of 12 feet.

CHINESE EVERGREEN (AGLAONEMA CRISPUM 'DEBORAH')

This easy-to-care-for plant can help filter out a variety of air pollutants and begins to remove more toxins as time and exposure continues. Even with low light, it will produce blooms and red berries.

Bamboo palm (Chamaedorea sefritzii)

Also known as the reed palm, this small palm thrives in shady indoor spaces and often produces flowers and small berries. It tops the list of plants best for filtering out both benzene and trichloroethylene. They're also a good choice for placing around furniture that could be off-gassing formaldehyde.

HEART LEAF PHILODENDRON (PHILODENDRON OXYCARDIUM)

This climbing vine plant isn't a good option if you have kids or pets — it's toxic when eaten, but it's a workhorse for removing all kinds of Volatile Organic Compounds (VOCs). Philodendrons are particularly good at battling formaldehyde from sources like particleboard.

Peace lily (Spathiphyllum)

Shade and weekly watering are all the peace lily needs to survive and produce blooms. It topped NASA's list for removing all three of most common VOCs— formaldehyde, benzene and trichloroethylene. It can also combat toluene and xylene.

Chapter 4: Designing Your Urban Garden

Once you have chosen a site for your urban garden, you'll begin the preparation and design process. You'll need to consider what type of garden you're going to have (in your yard, in pots or containers, raised beds, etc.) and whether it will be grown in regular soil or compost. We are going to discuss different methods of designing and preparing your garden for rooftops, staircases and balconies.

Designing Your Balcony Garden

If you're planning to grow a garden on your balcony or patio, you'll need to take a look at the space and layout to determine where you place your plants and how many plants you'll be able to grow. Do you want to have a seating area or do you want to have a balcony that is filled with vegetation? If you live in an apartment building, there's management to consider, so it's important that you keep the garden non-cluttered and organized. As you begin shopping for plants and seeds, think about the purpose of your garden – is it to be decorated with beautiful flowers or will it consist of edibles? Having a balcony garden is great because it allows apartment dwellers to grow plants and it requires less maintenance (no weeding, fewer pests, no mowing and no soil to till).

DRAW A BLUEPRINT OF YOUR GARDEN

Take a piece of paper and draw a scaled down version of your balcony, then begin filling it in with furniture and plants. This will give you an idea of how much space you will have for either. It's important to be realistic – you can't have lots of pots and large chairs and table on a small patio. If you are limited in space, try to decide which is more important between your patio furniture or garden. You can have fewer plants and more seating space or less seating space and more plants.

Start off by purchasing a few things for your balcony and filling it in slowly. This will allow you to prevent overcrowding your balcony. If you decide to place chairs on your patio, make sure to purchase durable materials and fabrics that can withstand heat, sunlight and rain. You can even purchase fold-up chairs and tables, so that you can make the balcony look less full. It's good to have your larger plants on the inside and smaller plants on the outside, so that the small plants can get sunlight (unless they're shade-loving plants).

LIGHTING

Your balcony should have enough light to allow your plants to grow. What direction is your patio facing? Are there any buildings or structures that block sunlight majority of the day? These are elements of gardening that we can't control, but there are alternatives that you can use if you have insufficient lighting, such as artificial light if you want to grow plants that need full sun on a balcony that is partly shaded. You can purchase solar-powered or battery-powered grow lights that you can place around your balcony garden. This will be needed, since most balconies don't have outlets – plus, it'll save you money by not running up your power bill.

PROTECTING YOUR PLANTS FROM HARSH WINTERS

Unless you live in Florida, South America or another location where winters aren't as cruel, you'll need to protect your precious plants from the cold. If you are using container plants, you can bring them indoors. It's important to consider this while you're planning your balcony garden. You don't want to have to bring in too many plants. For the plants that you have to keep outside, you can cover them to lock out majority of the cold. However, you may want to consider having a planting season that is from spring to winter, giving you a break during the winter holiday months when you'll likely be too busy to maintain them.

As a special note, make sure that you have your balcony garden approved by your landlord. Some property owners don't want gardens in their buildings. If your landlord doesn't have strict guidelines for the balcony, then get started on making plans!

Five Balcony Gardening Mistakes to Avoid

Starting a garden on your balcony can be an exciting experience, but if you aren't careful, you could make things harder for yourself. Beginning balcony gardeners usually make these mistakes, but you don't have to! Read on to see how you can make your balcony a bit more stress-free.

Don't Use a Lot of Small Pots

If you were to use too many small pots for your smaller plants, your balcony will quickly start to look cluttered. Also, when you place plants in small pots, it will stunt their growth (unless they are naturally small). Instead, use larger pots to allow your herbs and flowers to grow big enough to produce the results you desire. In fact, you can even make or buy large plant containers to hold multiple plants. Some people use large wooden planters or rubber bins.

Not Providing Sufficient Drainage

The soil you use for your container plants should have lots of drainage and allow for healthy root growth. To help with the drainage, you should drill holes at the bottom of the pots. Since your plants are in containers, water doesn't drain out as it should, like it would if it were in the ground. You'll also need a medium that allows the water to permeate (such as potting soil). This will help to counter drowning and killing your plants. Insufficient drainage can cause mold and other fungi to grow. Take note that certain plants, such as cacti and succulents require a lot of drainage than others. Potting soil is the best for this garden setup, since it was created for the confinements of containers – don't use outside dirt because it may not have proper drainage.

Choosing the Wrong Plants

It goes without saying that the plants you choose for your urban garden should match well with the amount of space that you have available. For instance, you can't purchase plants that grow large when you are trying to grow them on a balcony. Do research on the different types of plants that are available and learn about the type of growing space they require. Do they spread along the ground like grapes? Or can they be confined in containers like tomatoes and basil. Then you have light and shade to worry about. Some plants require more sunlight and others need shade. If your balcony has a lot of sun or shade, you should go for plants that would prosper in those conditions.

Over or Under-watering Your Plants

Ensuring that your plants have sufficient water is very important. Beginner gardeners can sometimes get carried away and overwater their flowers and vegetables. This will cause them to drown and die. Keep in mind that container plants tend to dry up fairly quickly, especially when it is hot, sunny and/or windy.

Make sure to check on your potted plants daily to ensure that they aren't too wet or too dry.

NOT UNDERSTANDING PESTS AND DISEASE

A lot of beginner gardeners who use pots and containers don't know common plant disease and pests when they see it. By overlooking these problems, your garden could be overwhelmed with one or both and fail miserably. It's necessary to nip these problems in the bud as soon as you recognize them, so that your garden will survive. Some of the pests that you should look for include little green caterpillars, especially around tomatoes. If you notice brown spots on the tomato's foliage, this could be a sign of them attacking. This is commonly overlooked as nothing by beginners. The brown spots are contagious to your other tomato plants and could end up killing them. Also, if your tomatoes obtain blight fungus, the spores can infect your next year's crops.

To prevent this from happening, make sure to learn everything you can about the plants you're growing and the common diseases and pests that they can attract. Then learn how to defeat the problem before it infects the rest of your garden.

COMMON BALCONY GARDEN PROBLEMS

The common problems that balcony gardeners tend to have are with shade, space and debris. Shade is a problem that is hard to deal with – you're either lacking in shade or have too much of it. If you live in an apartment building that has buildings in front or a lot of trees, you can ask for the limbs to be trimmed or you can move to another apartment location. If there is too much sunlight, you can make shade for your container plants. The great thing about container plants is that you can easily move them around – use this to your advantage to help your plants get sufficient sunlight and/or shade.

Debris like fallen leaves, bird food (if you have a bird house) and other flying objects from trees around your building can litter your balcony floor. If you don't have an easy way to clean it up, then your garden will look messy. Make sure that you clean out the pots to avoid accumulation of such debris (certain debris can alter the pH level of your soil).

Lastly, the amount of space you have on your balcony is likely limited and this is an issue that can't really be fixed. The only way you can handle this problem is to either move to a place with a bigger balcony or design your garden to fit what you've got to work with. The smartest way to make use of your limited balcony space is to plant your garden vertically. You can build or buy shelves and use hanging plant containers. There are even trellises that you can place against the walls to grow vining plants, like tomatoes.

If needed, you should bring your plants indoors when weather becomes too harsh (windy, wet, cold, hot).

TIPS FOR GARDENS ON SHADY BALCONIES

If you have a balcony that gets more shade than sunlight, this doesn't mean that you have to give up on your idea of having an urban garden. Instead of trying to fight against your shady elements, you can work with it to make your garden really work. Here are some ideas for four types of shady balconies.

NORTH-FACING BALCONIES

If your balcony faces the north, and doesn't have trees or buildings blocking out sunlight, you can make use of all the sunlight you'll be getting for sun-loving plants. You can even set up your garden design to have your larger sun-lovers in front and smaller shade-lovers behind them, so that they get blocked from too much sun. There are usually certain areas of the balcony that will get more sunlight than others (usually the outer edge), so arrange your plants in areas that benefit them the most.

BALCONIES COVERED BY PINE TREES

When you have pine trees surrounding your balcony, you're going to have to deal with the extra shade and annoying pine needles that will litter your balcony floor. You don't want pine needles inside of your potted plants because it will turn the soil acidic. Make sure to remove them as soon as possible. If you don't have time to maintain your plants frequently, you can choose plants like astilbe, columbine, azaleas, bleeding heart, hosta and heuchera (along with some other perennials), which love acidic soil and shady conditions.

BALCONIES THAT ARE DAMP AND COOL

For the gardeners who live in areas of the world that aren't hot and dry, and have a balcony that faces the northeast, you can plant ferns and perennials that like shade. With that being said, you should avoid succulent plants and Cacti because they won't do well in these conditions.

BALCONIES THAT HAVE AWNINGS AND WALLS

When balconies are too dark, you should hang your sun-loving plants on awnings to help them capture sunlight. If you have plants that can't tolerate the outdoor conditions, you can bring them inside or on the inside of your balcony. Plants that grow well in low sunlight areas include spider plants, peace lilies, pothos and bush lilies. To spruce up your shady garden, you can grow variegated foliage, which have multicolored leaves.

There are perks that come along with having a garden on a shady balcony. During the warmer months, you can enjoy additional shade inside of your home, bringing down energy costs. Also, you won't have to water your plants as much, since there is less heat and sunlight to evaporate the water.

VERTICAL GARDENING

A great way to make the most of the available space you have on your balcony is to use vertical gardening. This can be used for rooftops as well. Vertical gardening is a method that uses beanpoles, trellises and fences to train plants to grow upwards. If you plant to grow vining plants like tomatoes, you can use trellises or beanpoles to make them grow upwards. This will give you more space to grow more plants.

Shelves and wall trays can also be used for vertical gardens. You can hang shelves for your potted plants and use wall trays as a way to grow plants vertically from the walls. The wall trays have pockets that contain soil, so you don't have to use pots.

Must-Have Tools for Balcony Container Gardens

Being prepared with certain garden tools is important for properly starting and maintaining your balcony container garden. The tools you need can be found at your local gardening store and they're inexpensive. Here is the checklist:

Gardening Gloves: You don't have to have gloves, but if you want to keep dirt from getting under your nails or have sensitivities to some plants, you can wear them for protection. Those who don't want to touch earthworms, snails or caterpillars can find gloves to be useful as well. Gardening gloves are also good for maintaining plants with thorns.

Watering Can: Unless you want to get creative with a jug, you can purchase a watering can that you can easily transport in and out of your apartment. The great thing about them is that they pour through holes, which makes it resemble rain and prevents overwatering in certain parts. If you choose to use a jug, cover the hole with your fingers, so that it won't gush out. Also, avoid splashing the leaves with water because this can cause fungi to grow.

Trowel: These will help make digging in dirt easier. They work faster and they're cleaner than using your own hands to loosen the dirt.

Pruners: Some people use scissors, but pruners are the best tool for cutting off dead foliage. The wet sap that comes out of the leaves will leave a residue that will cause your scissors to rust. Pruners will minimize the risk of your plants becoming infected after being cut, since they offer a clean cut. They can also be used for plants that have thick stems.

Organic Pesticide: If you're interested in growing an organic garden, you're going to need organic pesticide to keep hazardous pests away. A lot of people squirm at the thought of plucking or killing caterpillars and other larger insects that commonly infest gardens. Non-organic pesticides can also be used, but spraying this on edibles can be a problem because you're going to have to consume the poison you sprayed onto them.

String and Sticks: This can be used for container plants that need a bit of help growing, such as tomatoes. Some plants need support as they grow and you can use these to do so.

Fertilizer: You can buy this in inorganic or organic form and in either a liquid or solid state. Make sure to get the right type of fertilizer for the type of plants that you'll be growing. Some need higher concentrations of phosphorous or nitrogen than others, so make sure to research your plant thoroughly.

How to Build a Cheap Shelf to Maximize Balcony Space

If you want to create more space on a tiny balcony, you can do so by building a cheap and easy shelf. All you need to do this is:

Six cylinder blocks

Four long pieces of thin wood (whatever size you choose)

All you have to do is place the wood on top of the cylinder blocks and you have yourself a usable shelf for your potted plants.

Designing a Gorgeous Stair Garden

If you have no balcony or want to use more space for your garden, you can use the stairs to your apartment as a garden (if you don't have to share it with other residents). Of course, you should speak with your apartment superintendent first. A lot of apartment buildings have outdoor stairs that can be used to grow all types of plants, including flowers, herbs and veggies. With a stair garden, you can use containers for your plants.

Unless you have wide stairs, you should set your smaller potted plants along one side of the steps. This will allow sufficient walking space to prevent accidental falls and visitors from knocking over your plants. It's best to use smaller sized pots because large pots may topple over. Avoid placing a pot on each step – skip a step or two instead. This will make your stairs look less crowded.

The plants you choose for your stair garden shouldn't grow too large to where it's hard to walk around them. Ferns are a good example of a plant that you don't want to have on your stair garden. Instead, you should go for herbs and short flowers like pansies, geraniums, petunias and impatiens.

If there is a wall that runs along your stairs, you can make use of climbing plants like English ivy and morning glories. These will cover the walls, giving it a nice design. Some even plant morning glories to add some color. There are a variety of other plants that you can train to grow vertically, such as tomatoes. If you don't have a wall, avoid using trellises because it could end up toppling over and damaging your garden. On the other hand, if you have an iron railing running up your stairs, you can use that for vining and climbing plants.

WARNINGS TO KEEP IN MIND

A stair garden can be a good idea, but there are some things that you should keep an eye out for that could reduce the quality of your plants. For instance, you should check with your apartment manager to ensure that they inform you before maintenance work is done around your garden. This will give you time to cover your plants or move them, so that they don't get contaminated.

There are instances where vandalism and theft can take place with stair gardens. It is possible for someone to take your potted plants or break them. There's little that you can do about this, but just keep this in mind if you decide to start a stair garden.

DESIGNING A ROOFTOP GARDEN

Rooftop gardens are a great option if you live in an apartment building that isn't utilizing that space. In some metro areas, it is uncommon to find balconies in apartment buildings, making it more ideal to use the rooftop instead. The rooftop of apartments are there for recreational and aesthetic purposes, but make sure to ask before starting a garden, especially if you want to use a large space. You can get signatures from tenants in the building to help get approval for a large rooftop garden.

There are many benefits behind having a rooftop garden. For one, it can absorb rainwater, insulate the apartment building and lower the temperatures. It will also create a wildlife habitat, which is uncommon in urban jungles. You can easily create a container garden that is maintainable and fruitful.

You may have heard of a couple of famous rooftop gardens in New York City, such as the Trump Tower public garden or the Rockefeller Center gardens.

When planning out your rooftop garden, you will need to:

- Get approval from the building owner
- Find out the weight capacity of the roof (hire a contractor to help you design the garden to fit those constraints)
- Use lightweight plant containers
- Set up windbreakers to block the high winds that are common at high altitudes. Windbreakers are designed to keep out wind, but allow sunlight to get through.

- Decide how you will set up the irrigation system. You can harvest rainwater and have a watering system installed that will automatically water your plants. This will keep maintenance low.

- Another way to design a rooftop is with raised beds, but make sure that having them won't be too heavy for the rooftops weight limit.

GROWING YOUR GARDEN INDOORS

Worst case scenario, if you don't have any outdoor space, or if you want more planting space, you can grow your garden indoors. Indoor gardening is ideal for those who have insufficient sunlight for a balcony or stair garden. Some people start seeds inside their home and then transplant them outdoors (such as peppers, tomatoes and other short-lived plants). Short-lived plants are the best to start with because if things don't go well and you want to discontinue gardening, just don't replant seeds.

On the other hand, if you will be starting long-lived plants that love sunlight, you will need to find them a place out on your balcony or windowsill. If you have a shady balcony, then you will need to find another location for them or try growing shade-loving plants.

HAVING SUFFICIENT LIGHTING FOR YOUR PLANTS

One of the most important aspects of indoor gardening is having proper lighting and enough of it. This will be a more expensive venture for urban gardening, but it'll be well-worth it when you're able to create enough vegetables and culinary herbs for your household. You're going to need overhead fluorescent tube lights that are made specifically for plant growth, such as aquarium lights. You can also buy the ones that are used for greenhouses.

If there isn't a place in your home where you can hang the fluorescent lights, you can use compact fluorescents, known as CFLs. These have a natural daylight color (check the packaging to make sure). These aren't the greatest lights to use for container plants because their intensity fades. Tube fluorescent lights are the best for container plants. These will produce sufficient lights for your plants for about 12 months. CFLs will give light for a growing season, but will have to be switched out regularly. Keep in mind that just because you see light doesn't mean that the intensity is there. When there intensity decreases, you can use them in lamps inside of your home.

It's a good idea to have your container plants near a window, even if it is facing north or has trees or buildings shading it. Your indoor plants will need all of the light they can get. If space allows, you can place your potted plants outdoors during the morning and afternoon, then bring them inside before the sun sets. You can turn off your grow lights when doing this to help save energy.

As your container plants begin to grow bigger, they will need lighting to be placed higher. Make sure that you install lighting that can be moved upward easily. Keep a close eye on your plants because certain ones grow fast. You don't want your plants to be too close to the lamps, which can leave them burned and damaged. To make your setup easier, you can purchase shop lights that have clamps. Just clamp them up on a stake that's sticking out of the container's soil. Then move it up higher and higher as it grows. Make sure to research the plant to determine how close the light should be from the plant (usually 12 to 18 inches away) and the type of lights it needs (full spectrum, red, white, etc.).

A good idea is to have the lights on a timer, so that you won't have to remember every day to turn them off and on. Between 10 and 12 hours of light is sufficient for most plants, but check the details about your plant to see how much light and shade it requires.

AIR, WATER AND HEAT

To ensure that your indoor plants are getting an atmosphere that resembles the outdoors, you're going to need to provide proper air circulation, heat and water. Here is what you can do to create a great atmosphere for your indoor container plants:

Air Circulation: Since you have four walls and a ceiling surrounding your plants, they won't be able to get the outdoor breeze that they require. To help with this, you can install a small fan that blows 24-7. You can set it to low and to rotate, so that it isn't constantly blowing on any one plant. Circulation helps plants to grow and minimizes the chances of fungi and garden pests.

Water: It's important that you don't overwater your potted plants because this could cause garden pests and fungus to grow in your soil. You'll notice gnats and flies if so. When this happens, you can use a fly trap. Make sure to allow the water to dry out. Your containers should have sufficient drainage. You can place trays beneath them to capture the water. The soil should also allow good absorption.

Heat: Depending on how many plants you decide to grow inside of your home, the amount of lights you have will give off heat, making the area warm. Keep this in mind when figuring out a place to set them. You may not want them too close to a spot where you like to rest because it can get too warm. Also, make sure that the temperature is alright for the type of plants that you're growing.

If you're worried about your electric bill, you can find energy efficient fluorescent light bulbs that you can use as grow lights.

Don't Forget About Weather

Depending on where you live in the world, you'll have to safeguard your plants from certain weather patterns. For instance, if you live along the coast, you could be susceptible to hurricanes and tropical storms. You can place plastic or Styrofoam sheets over your plants to protect them from the wind. You can also bring some inside until the storm is over. If you live on the first floor and fear floods, you can build shelves to place pots of plants on top of. Some people place bags of sand around their plant beds to help keep out raising waters.

While choosing a site for your garden, keep in mind sunlight, layout of the space and the types of plants you plan to grow.

CHAPTER 5: PREPARING THE SOIL FOR YOUR URBAN GARDEN

Having the correct soil for your plants is very important. You'll need to make sure that you use a medium that allows for root growth and proper drainage. The soil should also have lots of nutrition and the correct pH level (some plants require acidic soil and others alkaline soil). You will need to research the types of plants you want to grow to determine the best type of soil to use for them. Here, we will discuss the different types of nutrient-rich mediums.

WHAT IS POTTING SOIL?

Potting soil is commonly used in urban and above-ground gardening. It can be used for raised beds or container plants. It can be purchased a local garden center. A lot of people wonder why they can't just use the dirt that is outside of their home, and there are many reasons why they probably shouldn't. Unless you live in a rural area with rich soil, you're dealing with dirt that has insufficient drainage, pollution and a lack of nutrients (from not being planted in for so long and the lack of wildlife). Urban dirt is probably one of the most toxic forms of soil, so you want to avoid using that for your urban garden.

Potting soil is actually a soil-less mix that is made up of peat moss, ground pine bark, perlite, vermiculite and nutrients that's been added from slow-releasing fertilizers. You'll be able to buy a potting soil that is specifically made for the type of plants that you want to grow (veggies, rose flowers, bulbs, etc.). But don't let this confuse you. You can use regular potting soil for most plants, but succulents and cacti will need a mix that has additional sand. Then there are orchid flowers that should be planted in peat.

The reason why potting soil is used is because it is porous enough to allow sufficient drainage. The particles inside of it are between 1/16 and ¼ an inch in size. You don't want a medium that has particles that are too small because it will make the soil too dense to where the drainage is poor. Then if the particles are too large, it will retain too much water. When you are using container plants, it's necessary that excess water drains quickly. For soil to be proficient, it should be able to hold twice its own weight in water and absorb water fast. Potting soil doesn't swell or shrink when water is added or when it dries up. If the soil pulls away from the plant container when it is dry, then you will need to get better quality potting soil.

The pH level of your potting soil is important, but you won't have to worry about it until after you've been using it for a couple of years. The pH level will be affected by the fertilizers and type of water you use for your plants (if you use tap water, it may be hard or alkaline). The potting soil should be between 5 and 8.5 in pH level, outside of those levels will cause nutrient deficiencies. You can buy a pH level test kit, which are affordable, at your local garden shop. If the soil is too acidic or alkaline, you can adjust it with additives.

A lot of first-time gardeners like potting soil because you don't have to worry about annoying weeds, garden pests and fertilizers. It's common to buy soil that comes with insect eggs, but you'll rarely have this with potting soil.

TYPES OF FERTILIZER FOR YOUR SOIL

There are a variety of fertilizers that you can use for your soil. Fertilizer is used to make your soil richer in nutrients, which allows your plants to grow large and strong. You can choose between organic and inorganic fertilizers. Organic fertilizer comes from living organisms, while inorganic fertilizer comes from manmade chemicals.

ORGANIC FERTILIZERS

Many people find organic fertilizers to be the best option for gardening. They're natural and rich in nutrients. This includes manure, compost, worm castings and seaweed. Here's a look into the difference between them:

Manure: This is animal manure that is commonly mixed with sawdust or straw. It is rotted before being sold at local gardening stores.

Compost: This is made up of decomposing waste (kitchen and garden scraps like veggies and leaves). The bacterium that breaks down the contents makes it safe to be used in plant soil. If you're making your own compost, you can tell if the bacteria are working if the air around the pile fills warm.

Seaweed: This comes from the ocean. It is dried up and prepared at local garden shops. It is rich in potassium, which is great for plants. However, this isn't a balanced fertilizer.

Worm castings: This is like compost, but it uses the help of worms to break down the waste. This is commonly referred to as "black gold". You can make this yourself in your apartment for your balcony garden. It's great for the environment and helps plants to flourish.

INORGANIC FERTILIZERS

Your other option for fertilizer is the inorganic kind. This consists of chemicals and is made by man. It has additives like potassium, phosphorous, iron, nitrogen, magnesium, calcium, zinc and others. You can buy this from your local gardening store as well. It can be purchased in the form of liquid or solid. With liquid fertilizer, the nutrients are released fast, while pellets and granules release the nutrients more slow. With the solid form, you only have to add it once every month or season.

There are varying NPK (nitrogen, phosphorous and potassium) levels inside of inorganic fertilizers. You can check these levels by reading the labels of the package, which are represented by numbers separated by colons (4:4:6). The one you choose will depend on the plants that you're growing. For instance, if you want to have more leaf or stem growth, then you'd go with one that has a high nitrogen level. Then if you want more root growth, then you'd go with a fertilizer with a higher phosphorous level. For fruits and flowers, you can go with a fertilizer that has a high potassium level.

Although you can purchase a balanced fertilizer for majority of your plants, certain ones will require specific fertilizer types (like bromeliads and roses). You can find fertilizers that are labeled for specific plants.

TIPS FOR CREATING YOUR OWN COMPOST

If you're planning to use organic compost for your garden, why not learn how to make it yourself? There's nothing really to it and you could end up saving lots of money in the end. Creating your own compost gives you the control over what's placed in your soil. Knowing exactly what's decaying in the pile is important to some people who want to have a completely organic, healthy fertilizer.

THE BEST AND WORST ITEMS TO COMPOST

Having the right waste in your compost pile is very important. It isn't a trash can, so you don't want to put just any ol' thing inside of it. For instance, you want to avoid placing hazardous waste, plastic (even bioplastic), aluminum, glass, meat, oily stuff, dairy and fish into it. Your best bet is to use waste that you wouldn't mind consuming yourself (or actually do consume), such as scraps from vegetables, fruits and plants. If you drink coffee, you can even throw the leftover grinds in the pile.

Earth worms are also a great addition to the compost pile. Some people place shredded paper and cardboard in the compost pile, which is broken down by the worms. Yard and garden waste can be added, including leaves and sticks. If it was once alive and grew from the ground, you can consider putting it into your compost pile.

Overall, the best compost pile is one made by the gardener. It will reduce the amount of waste that you produce and will put it to good use. Try out different types of scraps to see which breaks down the best and that isn't too expensive for you to obtain regularly. As you harvest your garden, throw away the scraps into the pile right away. As a rule of them, your compost pile should be two parts browns (shredded paper, cardboard, sticks etc.) and one part greens (kitchen scraps, leaves, etc.).

If your compost pile is too dry, just add more water and if it's too wet, you can add more browns.

How Often to Add Compost to the Pile

Try to start your compost pile as soon as you can. Thereafter, you can add to the pile whenever you have scraps. It's good to add about an inch or so every couple of months when the soil level has decreased. If you eat a lot of vegetables and fruits, having enough compost shouldn't be a problem for you.

SHOULD YOU BRING IN YOUR BIN WHEN IT GETS TOO HOT OR COLD?

If you live in a location that has cruel summers and/or winters, you may be worried about your compost pile. The good news is that you don't have to bring your compost bins inside when the weather becomes too hot or cold. However, if you have worm bins, these should come inside, so that the worms don't die. To help with bug problems, you can set up a fruit fly trap or get organic pesticides (safe for worms) that will keep them out.

TOP WAYS TO CREATE YOUR OWN COMPOST AT HOME

Living in the city means having a small space for your garden and composting. If you have a balcony container garden, you can still enjoy the benefits of creating your own compost at home. You'll only need a small area of your balcony to contain your compost. There are a couple of composting methods that urban gardeners can use:

Compost Tumbler: This can be purchased online or at a local gardening supply store. It is a bit pricy, but they are very clean and easy to rotate your compost. It's also pest resistant. It's important to keep an eye on the amount of moisture that's inside of the tumbler because it's easy to saturate the pile. It takes about three to four months for the compost to be complete, depending on how often you tumble it.

DIY Composting Unit: All you need to create your own composting unit is a garbage can or bucket, a couple of bricks, a drill and a basin. Holes will have to be drilled at the bottom and the sides of the bucket or can. Then place it on top of the bricks and have a bowl beneath the bucket or can to capture excess water that flows out. A layer of sawdust or straw can be placed at the bottom of the can or bucket to help absorb water. Each day, add in your scraps and cover it with leaves or potting soil and a little bit of water. This may not be the easiest way of composting, but it's fast and affordable.

Anaerobic Composting: Some people find this method to be interesting and fun. It uses anaerobic bacteria, which is activated by absence of oxygen. All you have to do is fill a garbage bag with about 1/3 soil, 1/3 food scraps and 1/3 shredded leaves, grass or shredded paper. Then add water to the mix and tie the bag. This should be done when it isn't too cold. In about six weeks, you'll have compost.

Hopefully, these composting tips will help make your gardening easier and more affordable. You'll be able to plant your flowers and vegetables in the compost itself or by mixing the compost with your medium of choice (potting soil, etc.). The easiest method is the tumbler, but the other two are more affordable.

Chapter 6: Properly Watering Your Urban Garden

Water is the element of life and ensuring that your plants are getting enough of it is very important. When you water the soil of a plant, the roots drink the water and deliver it to the other areas of the plant. Some water is taken in through the leaves, but make sure not to drop water on the leaves of plants that tend to rot from water exposure. Since you will likely be using pots for your urban garden, you're working with a little bit of soil for the plants to draw water from. With that in mind, you're going to have to keep a close eye on whether you're under-watering or over-watering your garden plants. When the weather is windy, sunny and/or hot, make sure that you check your plants often to ensure that they aren't too dry.

If you have a balcony garden, make sure that the water in the pots are cycling through the container, instead of sitting on the surface. Once the water has drained through and the extra water drains away and the soil becomes dry, allow the plant to soak up the excess water from the tray for about 30 minutes. After that, remove the excess water, so that the roots don't become soggy. In case you overwatered your plant, just tip the pot over a bit and allow the water to run off.

When your soil is too dry, a gap will be created between the side of the pot and the plant. Before watering this plant, poke holes into the soil to allow the water to go through. Otherwise, the water will seep down the sides of the pot, draining out without the soil soaking it up for the plant to drink.

TIPS FOR WATERING YOUR PLANTS

There are a couple of ways you can ensure that your urban garden gets the proper water that it needs:

Choosing the Right Plant Containers: It's important that you choose a plant container that has a nice shape and construction. You want the shape and material of the pot to allow proper drainage. For instance, terra cotta containers have plenty of pores and allow the soil to dry out quickly. You should go with a wide-rimmed pot because they tend to dry out fast compared to pots with less surface area of soil.

Buy Plastic Plant Containers: Plastic containers are the best to use for your urban garden. When you have plant pots or hanging containers that have coconut lining, the water will dry out too quickly. If you decide to use these containers, make sure to place a plastic bag inside before placing the potting soil inside to help with insulation and to prevent too much loss of moisture. Holes should be punched into the bag, so that water can drain through.

Grow Proper Container Plants: It's important that you grow plants that can be placed in a container. You should also grow plants that are accustomed to your area of the world. For instance, if you live in a drought-prone area, you should grow plants that can sustain those conditions.

Water Plants at Night: A lot of people only think to water their plants during the day, but the best time to water container plants in is the evening and early morning hours. This will allow the plant's roots to soak up the water before the sun peaks over the horizon.

Place Mulch in the Containers: To help reduce the amount of water that evaporates from the surface, you can place mulch or pebbles on top.

Place Plant Containers Out of the Sun: It's a good idea to place your potted plants in areas that aren't too sunny. Doing so will cause the water to dry up fairly fast, requiring you to water it more often. You can place the containers in a shady part of your balcony.

Buy Water-Retaining Crystals: There's such a thing as crystals that can be used to retain water. You place them in your soil and it allows moisture to stay there, so that your plant can drink the water.

It's important that you keep an eye on your urban garden. Stick your fingers into the soil to determine if it has dried up and needs more water (up to the second joint on your finger). Sometimes the surface looks dry, but there's water in the middle. In this case, no additional water is needed yet. If you notice plants that are wilted, water them right away.

Chapter 7: How to Choose Plant Containers

Starting an urban garden can be done using plant containers. There are a variety of pots and containers that you can choose from, so it's important that you choose ones that will give you the best results (drainage, soil surface area, etc.). Plastic plant containers tend to be the best for balcony gardens because they're affordable, light-weight, durable and nice looking. You can find these containers at local garden shops. However, you can use just about anything that can hold potting soil and that you can drill holes into for drainage. Here is a look into the different types of containers you can use for your urban garden.

Terra Cotta Plant Containers

One of the most popular plant containers that you can buy are terra cotta pots. These are attractive and affordable. Other than that, these are reasons why you shouldn't purchase them for balcony gardens:

- The large containers are too heavy.

- They crack easy when temperatures drop too low (they may need take them inside and overwinter them)

- They break easily when you knock them over.

- Moving them around can be a pain because they are heavy and brittle (especially when moving to a new home).

- Since the containers are porous, a lot of moisture escapes from the soil.

If you really adore the terra cotta plant containers, you should go with plastic plant containers that resemble them. There are many out there that mimic their style, but some have a bigger price tag.

NURSERY POTS

It is very common for balcony container gardeners to use black plastic plant containers, rather than going with the more expensive pots. You may hear some gardening experts say not to use these pots. These containers are cheaper, but because they're black, it attracts more heat, which means that your soil will dry up faster. It can also make the roots of your plants too hot, stunting their growth. When you visit a plant nursery, you'll see them inside of these pots (hence the name nursery pots). By keeping them, it reduces the amount of plastic waste being hauled off to the dump. If you choose not to use them, you can donate them to a local garden shop or someone who uses them. Even recycle yards will take them.

For those who decide to keep the nursery pots, you may find few to no problems at all (unless you live in a hot climate or where there's a lot of sunlight on your balcony). One great thing about nursery pots is that they last for a very long time, even in hot weather and hot sun. So if you live in Arizona, you can use these with no problem (however, you may want to use nursery pots that have a lighter color).

CONTAINERS WITH FIBROUS LINING

Plant containers that have coconut fiber lining and other fibrous lining made from sphagnum moss are the first to suffer from heat waves and dry air. These pots may look attractive, but you should avoid those that have fibrous lining because moisture from the soil will escape on all sides. However, if you are still interested in these pots, you can place a plastic bag inside before putting in the potting soil. Make sure to poke holes into the bag.

Another option is to cut slits into different angles around the pot and then plant seeds (such as strawberries) to grow there. This creates a gorgeous look, sprouting strawberries from all angles. You can also do this with flowers. If you choose strawberries, plant them scarcely, because they will fill out the soil as they grow. The plants you grow inside will insulate the soil and help to lock in moisture.

METAL PLANT CONTAINERS

You'll find some urban gardeners using metal containers for their balcony. They are aesthetically pleasing and light on the pockets. The great thing is that you can make this yourself using coffee cans or large food cans that are thrown out by restaurants. The only issue with these is that they can blind you when the sun reflects off of them. They also accumulate rust stains on the balcony's surface as they grow old.

PLASTIC PLANT CONTAINERS

The best plant containers that you can find today are those made from plastic. They're inexpensive and they have a variety of shapes and sizes to choose from. Plastic plant containers offer great drainage, while still retaining moisture in the potting soil. Then to top it off, they're lightweight, which is something you should be looking for if you are growing your garden on a balcony or if you plan to move your plants around often. An alternative to buying containers is to use plastic food containers – just paint them to give them style.

RECYCLED PLANTING POTS

If you are looking for an eco-friendly solution for your urban garden, you can go with recycled pots. You can use anything from old paint cans to coffee cans. When choosing which containers to recycle, you should consider its durability to weather elements, whether you're able to drill holes into it for drainage, if it is aesthetically pleasing and if there are dangerous sharp edges (like on a can that's been opened with a can opener or knife). Other questions you'll want to ask is if it will ruin the floors of your balcony and if the plant inside can be repotted easily in the future. You may want to consider whether you want your whole garden to have the same containers and whether you can accommodate that. Some people use large storage bins as recycled containers. Even plastic bags can be used for plants like potatoes and other vegetables that need lots of dirt.

Recycled Styrofoam plant containers can be used for urban gardens. Containers recycled from plastic storage bins and soda bottles will break down after being exposed to sunlight and water for too long. If you want a recycled container that will maintain its quality and durability, then you should consider using Styrofoam (polystyrene). If the container is large enough, you could use it for the long term.

Chapter 8: DIY Self-Watering Plant Containers

When it's hot out, you'll end up having to water your plants multiple times a day. This can become time consuming for some people, but there is another option. You can even use this if you're planning to go on vacation for a couple of days and don't have anyone to water your plants. If you have a balcony garden that uses plant containers, you can use watering bulbs in all of the pots.

What You Need for a Self-Watering Container

Some people purchase self-watering containers, but if you want to do it yourself, you're going to need:

- A new plant container

- Lantern wicks

- Peat moss

If you currently have a lot of plant containers, you can double-pot them. To do this, you'll need to find one that is around 4 inches bigger in diameter. It shouldn't come with any drainage holes at the bottom. You'll place your smaller container inside of this one to give the illusion that it is just one container. Some people use nursery pots for the inside container.

First, you'll need to place the peat moss at the bottom of the larger container, and then place the planted container inside of it. Then to fill up the sides, place peat moss there. Cut the lantern wick that you have into several lengths, then place one end several inches into the soil of your plant container and the other end into the peat moss of the larger container. If you have a large container, use a couple pieces of wick. Afterward, put water in the outer container and the lengths of the wick will soak up the water and distribute it to your plant soil.

This watering system will trickle water into your plant's soil for a couple of days, keeping it moist.

TIPS FOR KEEPING YOUR CONTAINER PLANTS HEALTHY

Growing an urban garden with container plants doesn't have to be difficult. With the right knowledge, you can successfully grow container plants on your balcony, rooftop or even inside of your home. Keep these tips in mind to help ensure that you get the best results from your flowers, fruits, vegetables and/or herbs.

Don't overwater your plants: It's easy to overwater your potted plants when you're new to gardening. It's important that you not put too much water at one time or water your plants too frequently. When you overwater your plants, the roots won't be able to get enough oxygen and will begin to rot. It can also cause mushrooms and fungi to grow.

Don't let your plants get too dry: Overwatering is a more common problem, but some beginner gardeners allow their plants to dry out. This is a problem, especially when it is hot and sunny outside. During the summer, it's important that you keep your plants' soil moist and provide the plants with shade, so that their leaves don't burn.

Use potting soil for your plants: When planting your edibles and non-edibles in containers, it's best to use potting soil, especially for balcony gardens. Regular garden soil tends to become compact when it's placed in a container, which decreases drainage and root growth. Potting soil will lock in moisture and provide your plants with proper room for roots to sprout.

Give your plants plenty of light: Whether you're growing your plants indoors or outdoors, it's important that your plants get enough light. If you will be growing on a balcony that has a lot of shade, you're going to have to plant those that don't need lots of light. If you happen to be facing south, your balcony could get very hot, drying out your plants. Make sure to provide enough shade and water if so.

Give your plants large enough containers: It's important that your plants are in containers that are large enough for them. For instance, you can't plant large flowering plants like bird of paradise inside of a container that is only 3 gallons. Keep in mind the weight limit of your planting space, so that you don't have too many large containers on it.

Learn how to identify pests and disease: To keep your potted plants healthy, you're going need to know when they are being attacked by disease and pests. A small amount of pests are alright, but when there is an infestation, you'll need to get rid of them. It's best to start eliminating them as soon as you notice them. The same goes for diseases – nip the problem in the bud.

Fertilize your soil: Potting soil doesn't come with a lot of nutrients, so you're going to have to add fertilizer to it. This is especially so after two years when the potting soil will be fully depleted of all nutrients. To add compost your container, use vermicomposting bin. This will enable your plants to grow quicker and healthy. You can choose to add a liquid fertilizer weekly or a solid fertilizer monthly. Make sure not to add too much fertilizer because it will burn the roots. It's best to add fertilizer when the plants are actively growing, not when they're dormant.

Bring in sensitive plants during the winter: If you leave weaker container plants outside during the winter, they are likely not to survive. Bring them indoors until it starts to get warm again.

Don't rush your plants growth: It's common for beginning gardeners to be impatient with their garden. Many rush seedlings to sprout or for a flower to bloom, but it all takes time. Don't pluck them too soon and don't give up. As long as you are maintaining your garden well, your plants will grow great.

Be realistic about your garden: When you first start your garden, it's important that you be realistic about the setup and capacity of the garden. Don't try to overdo it if you only have limited space. Also, make sure that you're able to grow the type of plants that you want to grow in the region that you live in.

CHAPTER 9: HOW TO START SEEDS INDOORS

If you're just starting out your urban garden, you're going to need to figure out how and where you're going to start your seeds. It's very common to start seeds indoors, which is usually done before the last frost comes (between February and March). This will get things moving along, so that when spring arrives, you can place your already-budding plants outdoors. You can either purchase a seed starting kit or just use a homemade one using an egg carton with drainage holes at the bottom. Just set the egg carton on top of a tray or plastic bag, so that the excess water is captured.

Keep in mind that not all seeds have to be started indoors. Some you can go ahead and plant into the soil of your outdoor containers and they will sprout just fine (such as sunflowers, columbine, poppies and a variety of others). Plants that you will need to start indoors include petunias, broccoli, peppers, snapdragons, marigold, coleus, lettuce, tomatoes and zinnias.

It can't be stressed enough how important it is to first research the plants that you plan to grow, so that you can know exactly how to start their seedlings. This information is usually on the back of the seed packet. It will let you know the planting depth, how long it takes to germinate and how far apart they have to be planted from one another. Some seeds have to be soaked in water before being placed in potted soil. Others need to be placed in warm (using heating pad) or cool (using refrigerator) temperatures before being planted.

It's necessary to only sow seeds that are fresh (those under one year old or have been kept in great conditions) or they may not sprout. Some people use a wet paper towel to wrap the seeds in, which is then placed inside of a Ziploc bag. There should be around 10 seeds per paper towel. Once they germinate, you can place them in your home-made or store-bought seed starting tray. This method will ensure that all of the seeds in the tray have sprouted, rather than wasting valuable space.

When it comes time to sow the seeds, place them inside of plant containers that are well-drained and contain seed-starting mix. You can use potting soil from your garden, but be wary of weeds or insects. It's best to use a fresh bag of potting soil to avoid this. Some choose to sterilize their old soil to get rid of fungus and disease (this is done by placing it in the oven on 180 degrees Fahrenheit for two hours). The soil should reach the top of your plant container, so that airflow reaches the sprouted seeds.

The seeds should be kept moist at all times until they germinate. Once they germinate, you will need to use room temperature water normally (don't overwater or underwater). If you will be using indoor lighting, make sure that they are placed about 12 inches from the seeds. If using sunlight, they should be kept in a south-facing window. When using natural sunlight, make sure to rotate the trays, so that the seedlings don't end up growing in the direction of the sunlight. You'll need to provide your seedlings with proper air circulation and temperatures as well (usually between 65 and 72 degrees Fahrenheit).

Once you see a couple of "true leaves" (the leaves that photosynthesize and have more of the characteristic of the plant that you're growing) come in, you can transplant them to a plant container and place them outside after the last frost.

The great thing about starting your seeds indoors is that it allows you to enjoy your plants longer and give you faster yields, than planting later in the spring.

USING RECYCLED MATERIAL TO START SEEDS

If you're looking for an eco-friendly way to start seeds for your urban garden, you can do so by using old toilet paper rolls, egg trays, plastic party cups, Starbucks cups and many other items. It's a good idea to plant a lot of seeds in small containers, so that you can get a higher yield of sprouts. The ones that do sprout can be transplanted to larger containers and placed on your balcony once it gets war. By using recycled material, you will be able to reuse items that you would have normally thrown away and then you can reuse them for as long as they survive. Just make sure to poke drainage holes at the bottom of whatever you decide to use. You will also need a waterproof tray (plate, takeout tray, etc.), unless you plan to use a surface that is waterproof, such as a kitchen counter. Don't forget to place them near a window or under grow lights for proper growth.

TRANSPLANTING SEEDLINGS TO OUTDOOR CONTAINERS

Once you have started your seeds, it will be time to get them prepared for transplantation. This is an important process that shouldn't be taken lightly. Like with surgery, if you don't carefully transplant the seedling, you could end up with dead seedlings. Here are a few tips you can use during the transplant process:

- Water the potted soil before the day you transplant the plant. By doing so, it will ensure that your seedlings get enough hydration after being transplanted. You don't want to place them in dried up soil.

- Put your plants in the containers outdoors when it isn't too sunny out. It's best to do it on a day that is overcast and cool, particularly during the evening hours.

- After transplantation, water the plant right away.

- Avoid having the roots exposed in the sun, wind or heat.

- Dig a hole into the container and place water inside, then place the plant inside.

- Once you have placed the plant into the container, fill the hole halfway with water and then allow it to settle into the soil and the plant's roots, then fill in the hole completely.

- Don't pat down the dirt around the plant. Just pat it lightly.

You should place the new plant in a shaded area, outside of direct sunlight, for about three to five days. You can place the pots in shaded areas of your balcony or rooftop if you don't have direct shade. Some people even place the pot indoors for the first week and then allow it to sit out on the balcony.

It's important that you regularly check your plants for the first couple of weeks. This will tell you if the transplant went well. Try to water the plants twice daily if it is hot out. Keep in mind the watering needs of the type of plant that you have transplanted because not every plant is the same.

TIPS FOR SAVING YOUR SEEDS

Now that you know how to start seeds and transplanting them, it's time to learn about saving seeds. Unless you plan on buying seeds every season, you can harvest seeds from your garden and reuse them for the next round. You can even give them to friends or sell them. Here are a couple of tips to help you with saving seeds:

Only pick the best seeds: It may be tempting to save all the seeds you can find, but not all seeds are worthy. For instance, if you have a tomato that didn't grow so well, you don't want to use the seeds because they're likely not fully developed. Take seeds from plants that grow large and healthily.

Dry the seeds you have picked: After you have picked the seeds you want to save, make sure to clean them off using a moist paper towel and then place them on a plate to dry. Seeds from a tomato will have a juice all over it, while bell peppers have dry seeds that don't need to be washed. Allow the seeds to dry for a day or two before you place them inside of a container that is airtight.

Place labels on the containers: Make sure to place seeds in separate containers and have them labeled. Store the containers in a cool, dry place. Some people use Ziploc bags. The label should also contain the date of harvest. Most seeds can be saved for about two years. After expiration, you can either toss them or try to plant them to see if they will sprout.

The more you save, the more you have: Keep up with saving seeds and you'll never have to buy seeds again. You'll be able to have control over how many seeds you have and the knowledge of where exactly the seeds came from. If you are planting an organic garden, this is very important because you can never be too sure whether seeds have had any contact with chemicals.

Chapter 10: Choosing Plants for Your Urban Garden

When it comes to deciding what plants you want to grow in your urban garden, you'll have to consider the region you live in, the space you have available and the amount of shade and sunlight your space receives. If you plan to grow indoors, you'll need to consider your budget for purchasing the items you need for the setup. Those who live in an apartment that has lots of sunlight on the balcony or rooftop won't have to worry about choosing between sun-loving or shade-loving plants. All you'll have to worry about is whether the plant can grow in the weather that your region has to offer. If you are struggling with a balcony that has a lot of shade, there are plants that you can grow without a problem.

Edibles that Grow on Shady Balconies

Having a shady balcony can still produce edible plants. A lot of fruits and vegetables require lots of sunlight, but if you can't have trees trimmed to allow more light, you can go with plants like mint, beans, peas, lettuce, cauliflower and spinach. Here is a list of other edibles:

- Chives
- Cardamom
- Parsley
- Small cucumbers
- Blueberries
- Currants
- Gooseberries
- strawberries

FLOWERS THAT LOVE THE SHADE

There are shade-loving flowers that you can plant on your shady balcony as well, including peace lilies, caladium bicolor plants, torenia, impatiens, coleus and perilla. It's a good idea to move your potted plants around your balcony to allow them to get as much sun as possible. Here is a list of others:

- Browallia
- Oxalis
- Polka-Dot Plant
- Fuchsia

- Sweet Potato Vine
- Lobelia
- Viola
- Balsam
- Beefsteak Plant

LIST OF SHADE-LOVING PLANTS

Here is a list of shade-loving plants:

- Pothos (Epipremnum aureum)
- Peace lily (Spathiphyllum floribundum)
- Bush lily (Clivia miniata)
- Spider plants (Chlorophytum comosum 'Variegatum')
- Primrose (Oenothera speciosa)
- Jacob's ladder (Polemonium caeruleum)
- Meadowsweet (Astilbe spp.)
- Virginia bluebell (Mertensia virginica)
- Columbine (Aquilegia spp.)
- Foxglove (Digitalis spp.)
- Flax lily (Dionella spp.)
- English ivy (Hedera helix)

- Coleus (Solenostemon spp.)

- Fuchsia (Fuchsia spp.)

- Impatiens species

- Variegated ground ivy (Glechoma hederacea 'Variegata')

- Variegated lily turf (Liriope muscari)

- Bleeding heart (Lamprocapnos spectabilis, formerly classified as Dicentra spectabilis)

- Hosta (Hosta plantaginea)

- Solomon's seal (Polygonatum biflorum)

- Jumpseed (Persicaria virginata)

- Japanese anemone (Anemone hybrida)

- Azalea (Rhododendron spp.)

- Leopard plant (Ligularia spp.)

- Many types of ferns

VEGETABLES THAT LOVE CONTAINERS

If you're planning to grow vegetables in containers, you will find this list to be helpful in choosing which ones you'll grow in your urban garden:

- Beans

- Beets

- Bell pepper
- Broccoli
- Brussels sprouts
- Cabbage
- Carrot
- Cherry tomatoes
- Chicory
- Cilantro
- Cucumber
- Eggplant
- Garlic
- Jalapeno peppers
- Lettuce
- Lima beans
- Onion
- Potato
- Radishes
- Romaine lettuce
- Spinach
- Squash
- Swiss chard
- Tomatillo

- Tomato

There are many other plants that you can choose from that haven't been listed. Search around for plants that grow in your region and see if any of them fit what you're looking for. At the end of the day, the type of plants you choose for your urban garden should be based on what you want to yield from it. Do you want to have a lot of edibles to bring down your food bill? Or do you want to grow a garden that is filled with flowers and plants in order to decorate your patio or stairway?

The types of plants you choose should be based on the purpose that your garden will serve – to feed or to entertain.

CHAPTER 11: PROTECTING YOUR PLANTS FROM SUMMER AND WINTER

Having an outside garden means nurturing your plants when things get tough. During the summer and winter months, things may get too rough for your weaker plants, so you'll need to take certain measures to help your plants to survive.

PROTECTING YOUR PLANTS FROM HARSH WINTERS

Urban gardeners who live in areas where it gets really cold during the winter will need to take precautions to keep their garden alive. Some containers will do fine in cold temperatures, while others tend to expand, freeze or crack. If you have brittle containers that can't stand winter, make sure to bring these indoors. It's a good idea to purchase containers that can withstand winter temperatures at the time you design your urban garden. If you don't want to bring your plants indoors, you'll need plant containers that will overwinter well. Unless you live in a city where the temperature drops below 40 degrees (which is considered freezing), then you won't have to worry about overwintering your pots.

Which Pots to Bring Indoors and Which to Leave Outdoors

Certain types of plant containers will need to be taken inside when temperatures reach below freezing, such as terra cotta, glass and glazed plant pots. The pots that you're able to leave outside include Styrofoam, fiberglass, concrete, wood, plastic, polyurethane and hypertufa. If you decide to plant in containers that can sustain freezing temperatures, make sure you use them for plants that are cold-hearty (can withstand freezing temperatures). For annual plants, you can use the indoor pots like terra cotta, which can be stored in your home during their off season.

If space allows, you can keep the soil inside of your pots that you won't be using during the winter. Then reuse them next year. If the soil was stricken by disease, you will need to sterilize it before reusing it next season. If you have to keep your pots of soil outdoors, you can protect them by covering it with bubble wrap, which will lessen the chances of them breaking.

Your best bet is to buy plant containers that are able to withstand the cold temperatures that occur during the winter where you live. Being prepared is the best way to make your urban garden successful.

Ways to Overwinter Your Plants

Urban gardeners that have to deal with freezing cold winters should practice plant overwintering. If you don't want to have to worry about this task, you can plant annuals each spring on your balcony, so that you won't have to fret over winter gardening. You can plant evergreens that are made to withstand cold weather, while other plants can just be replanted the following season. On the other hand, you can use overwintering methods to keep things growing throughout the freezing season.

Grow Your Plants Indoors

During the winter, you can bring inside your weaker plans. You can make space for your plant containers by placing them on window sills and shelves on the wall. It's important that they get plenty of sunlight and are set away from cold drafts. If there isn't enough light inside your home, you can use artificial grow lights instead.

You may notice that your plants seem to be dying at first, but this is their way of adjusting to the new conditions. Just keep giving them light and water and they will bounce back to health. Place a small fan around your plants to improve air circulation. Don't overcrowd the plants – this will only promote pests and disease.

Take Cuttings Indoors

If you are growing herbaceous tropical plants that have soft stems, you may want to take its cuttings and allow the mother plant to perish outside. Bring the cuttings indoors and place them in a glass of water on a window sill. You will see its roots begin to grow. This will save you space, since you won't have to use plant containers.

ALLOW THE PLANT TO GO DORMANT

It's alright to leave some plants outside to go dormant during the wintertime. In fact, some plants will need this time to rest. When plants go dormant/die, their energy is stored under the soil in tubers. Once it becomes warm again, they will sprout back to life. Plants that are known to do this include cannas and caladium. The soil should be barely moist and the pot should be kept in a place that is cool and dark. Some people dig up the bulbs and wrap them in peat moss or a wet newspaper, then place them in a garbage bag. This is then placed inside of the home in a place that is cool and dry. It's important that the tubers remain at temperatures between 40 and 50 degrees Fahrenheit. Make sure to check on the bulbs monthly to see if they are firm and not dried out. Once spring comes around, you can replant the bulbs in plant containers inside your home before placing them back outside. This will give them time to acclimate gradually. Make sure to research the plant you have to see if it should be brought in before or after the first frost.

It's important to note that overwintering isn't a sure way to save your plants, but it can work in most cases .Some plants will fail because they're all different. You can learn more about the plants you have and how they should be overwintered. If you don't want to do this task, you can just plant new seeds every spring.

PROTECTING YOUR PLANTS FROM HARSH SUMMERS

The summer can be just as harsh as the winter, leaving your plants to wither away and die. When growing container plants, it can be even worse for your plants because they tend to dry up fairly quickly as it is and put hot summer heat on top of that and you'll have severe over-drying. Just one day of harsh heat can cause leaves of certain plants to fall off and crumble. Some plants will recover in a few weeks while others will die. It's important that you regularly check on your plants during the summertime, so that you can keep an eye on their health.

WATER YOUR PLANTS OFTEN

It's very important that you water your plants twice daily – once in the early morning and once in the early evening. The sun should not be in the sky when you water them, which is a good thing, since it won't be around to evaporate majority of the water. This will give your plants time to drink up the water you provide and survive through the high heat without drying out. Container plants tend to lose a lot of moisture. If you are growing plants like tomatoes, cucumbers and strawberries, it's important that they be kept well-watered.

Make Sure The Water Goes Deep

When watering your plants, make sure that the water trickles down slowly through the soil. If it is running out too fast, poke holes in the soil and pour the water to help it soak through the middle where the roots are. There should be a tray at the bottom of the plant container to catch excess water, some of which will be soaked up by the plant. After about 10 to 30 minutes, you should dump out this excess water to avoid fungi growth and overwatering.

Spray Your Plants With Water

Buy a spray bottle and use it to spray a mist onto your plants. This will keep the leaves from shriveling up from the dry heat. Make sure not to over-mist them, especially when it is humid outside because this can promote mold and fungus and other diseases to fester.

Give Your Plants Shade

Ensuring that your plants aren't bombarded with hot sunlight, it's necessary that you provide them with sufficient shade. You can do this by putting up a screen around your balcony (if approved by your landlord) or you can bring certain plants indoors. Just keep them in front of a bright window, so that they get their daily dose of sunlight.

Put Mulch In Your Containers

To help with insulating your plants from harsh summer heat, you can use mulch. Pebbles can also be used to help prevent water from settling at the top of the soil.

CHAPTER 12: COMMON INSECT PROBLEMS IN GARDENS

There are certain pests that you'll find in majority of gardens. The good thing is that urban gardens tend to have fewer types of pests, especially if you live on high story. But there are flying insects that can still get to your garden, giving you problems with infestations.

Aphids: These are small insects that are hard to detect unless you look closely. They are green and blend in pretty well with your plants. If you spot them, make sure to spray them with soapy water. If you notice certain leaves have been infected, clip them off with pruners and trash them. Try using predator insects to help combat them.

Ants: You know all about these little buggers and if you're not careful, you could have majority of your plants' foliage eaten up. Ants actually encourage aphid population and use them to produce a sticky sap that they love to eat. Soapy water can be used to spray them off as well.

Tomato hornworm caterpillars: These fat little bugs blend in well with your potato and tomato plants. They like to hang upside on plant stems, while they eat away all of your leaves. They sometimes get fatter than an index finger. You can pluck them off and put them on the ground. If you have ants, they will find it almost right away.

Cabbage looper caterpillars: These are similar to the hornworm caterpillars. They will eat your plants fast. They like to eat cabbage, so keep an eye out for damage to the plant's leaves. You should get these caterpillars as far away from your plants as possible or kill them

Snails and slugs: These slimy creatures love to eat plant leaves. You should get rid of them as you see them. Some people use beer traps to capture and kill them. Other people step on them, but that can be kind of gross.

Keep in mind that not all insects are bad for your garden. There are many that are actually beneficial, such as butterflies, bees and grass skippers. You can even use praying mantises and lady bugs to combat pests that are eating up your garden. You can purchase beneficial bugs at your local garden shop. You may also want to get earth worms to place inside of your compost and potted plants.

CHAPTER 13: WHAT IS AEROPONICS?

There is another way that you can grow your urban garden and that's with an aeroponic setup. Aeroponics is a method of growing plants without using any type of medium (no soil or water). This form of growing plants is oftentimes confused with hydroponics, which uses water instead of soil. You will find a variety of products being sold that uses this form of growing. They come in the form of towers. More and more people are using aeroponics because it is fast, energy efficient and grows plants quickly.

HOW AEROPONICS GARDENING WORKS

In an aeroponics tower, which consists of frames or horizontal boards, the plants are placed inside of it, allowing the leaves and the roots to be suspended in the air. Little water is needed and no soil is needed at all. The seeds are started by spraying them with water that is filled with nutrients. The seeds begin to sprout and the system continues to spray this nutrient-rich water onto them. Eventually, you'll have a tower of plants that have exposed roots and foliage, allowing you to easily pluck your fruit and vegetables.

WHY USE AEROPONICS

There are many benefits associated with aeroponics gardening. As mentioned, it needs no soil and mists of nutrient-rich water, making it very eco-friendly. Because the plant and roots are suspended in air, it is able to give it plenty of oxygen. This form of gardening allows the plants to grow very fast (twice or triple as fast as soil gardens). You'll even notice more seeds being yielded from the plants. Since the plants aren't in soil, you won't have to worry about diseases and weeds. The water that is used is sterile, preventing disease from forming. Then the watering system doesn't overwater, which eliminates the worry of mold and fungus growth. You can place an aeroponics tower just about anywhere, including on your balcony, rooftop or even inside of your home. Aeroponics towers can be used to grow anything you want, including flowers, herbs, vining plants and vegetables.

HOW TO WATER AN AEROPONICS GARDEN

In an aeroponics garden, only 10% of the water soil requires is needed. An irrigation system is set up that automatically sprays a mist over the seedlings and plants. Careful attention should be given to the size of the water droplets that are being distributed. A lower-pressure system is commonly used to deliver the nutrients to the plants.

When the water droplets are too big, the plant won't receive as much oxygen. When plants receive droplets that are too tiny, it can cause it to grow excessive hair and prevent lateral root system growth. If this happens, the plant won't be able to grow as efficiently.

BUYING AN AEROPONICS SYSTEM

To get you started with aeroponics urban gardening, you will need to purchase a kit. You can find plenty of them on the Internet. The price tags for these towers can be high, but it is well-worth it. You'll be able to grow a lot more food more quickly and you won't have to use nearly as much resources, saving you money in the long run. You can learn about more affordable aeroponics systems on our Facebook page here: http://on.fb.me/HmllNU

After setting up your kit, according to the directions, you'll need to place the seeds in the pockets of the tower. A couple of days of misting them with nutrients will pass by before you start to see seeds sprouting. Those that don't, you can replace. Make sure to give the seeds enough time to germinate – some plant seeds take longer than others, so make sure you know how long to wait before deeming the seeds no good.

Once the seedlings start to grow, you will see the roots begin to expose themselves through the trays. Make sure to use pruners to trim the roots, so that they don't get entangled with the other plants. After your plants have matured, you can begin harvesting them.

CHAPTER 14. ENJOYING YOUR URBAN GARDEN

Having an urban garden can be a miracle in concrete jungles, but it isn't impossible. If you want to be able to provide more food for your family or grow beautiful flowers, even if you don't have the luxury of yard space, you can use urban gardening to your benefit. Hopefully, you have learned enough to help you get your urban garden started. You will find that there is a lot to learn along the way, so just take lessons learned to help you make things right the next time around.

The great thing about urban gardens is that the methods require little maintenance. The setups are pretty simple (unless you're trying to outdo Trump Towers' public garden) and affordable. All it takes is time and dedication to get your urban garden ready for production.

If you have children and family, try to get them involved. The more people there are to help you maintain the garden, the better. This will put less stress on your shoulders and will give everyone a learning lesson in agriculture.

There's nothing like walking out to your stairs, balcony or rooftop and plucking a tomato or basil leaves to cook in tonight's dinner. Not many people can say they have that in the city, but you can!

With the right tools and knowledge, your urban garden will flourish and who knows, you may have a green thumb. Don't be afraid to test things out. You can always start small and then slowly but surely add more plants to your setup.

Remember all of the tips that were presented in this e-book and it could help to save you a lot of headaches and money. Take pictures of your garden from beginning to harvest time and send it to your friends and family who live too far away to see it themselves. Maybe even post it to your blog or Facebook. You may inspire other city dwellers to delve into urban gardening.

You will learn a lot while urban gardening, but most of all, make sure to have fun with it!

Excerpt From The Container Gardening Book

Flowers That Love Containers

There are two types of flowers: (1) flowers which require full sun (require 6 or more hours of direct sun) to grow well, and (2) flowers which require shade to develop to their potential. You have here five examples of each type of flower that you could choose.

However, keep in mind that the best way to start is with plants that are least capricious but still beautiful. Both these attributes would encourage you to learn more about container gardening and promote your enthusiasm for increasing the number of your pots.

Sun Loving Plants For Your Container Garden

Millions Bells (*Calibrachoa*) – the million bells comes in about all imaginable colors from pure white to various shades of deep purple and pink. This is a flower that not only is easy to grow, but also looks great in almost any type of container indoor or outdoor. The delightful blossoms are known to attract bees and butterflies as well as the stunning hummingbirds. The blooms will go strong throughout the summer if you are careful about fertilizer and watering it will last half through the fall. These plants do require constant watering and a very good drainage; waterlogged soil would result in rotting roots and a dead plant.

Verbena (*Verbena officinalis*) – This is a hot favorite for those who love container gardens because this is one plant that will flower continuously throughout all summer and even a good part of the fall. It has an excellent presence and it will look good in any type of container as it will fill spaces and spill over edges covering the containers with its delightfully clustered blossoms.

This is a flower that comes in many colors of verbena, i.e. from bright red to deep - almost dark - blue. These long-term bloomers are extremely strong and unassuming. They will even survive drought as long as they have container with good drainage. You need to keep in mind that these flowers like most flowering plants, require the soil to be fertilized every 2-3 of weeks. To ensure that you have them flower continuously, you would need to remove the dead flowers. These flowers are great for attracting butterflies.

Cape Daisy (*Osteospermum*) - These plants are very hardy, bright and cheerful and come in wide variety of colors that range from a deep pink to purple, melon, and white.

They do not require you to remove the dead flowers as they will continue flowering unabated throughout the summer. However, the plants certainly will definitely look much better if you do remove them (dead flowers). They require regular fertilization and good drainage. If they have these two things, they will last well into fall.

Bush Violet (*Browallia*) – this flower will give some of the most wonderful blossoms with their rich blue color and velvety texture and wide smiling looks. This is a plant that will go well with almost everything. Owing to its height, which is about 12-14 inches, this is a great choice for planting in the center of a mixed container garden.

The Bush violet is happy all the time and requires least attention. It does require to be protected from too much wind, if you have any in your area. Another factor that is very important for the growth of this plant is drainage. With regular fertilization, this is a plant that will flower strongly and continuously throughout the summer and a good part of the fall as well.

Pentas (*Pentas lanceolata*) – also known as Egyptian Star Flower, this is another hot favorite in container gardens owing to their very beautiful clusters of star-shaped flowers. Butterflies and hummingbirds love these flowers, especially the red and dark pink varieties. They are happy with least care and will bloom even when exposed to drought and heat. It does need good soil, regular fertilizing and good drainage. If it has all that your pentas would happily bloom until the fall.

Shade Loving Plants For Your Container Garden

Fuchsia (*Fuchsia*) – it is believed that these flowers are a fussy lot, but this is not true. The fact is that these flowers are among the loveliest plants you can grow in containers in shade.

You will find that these flowers will bloom happily the whole of summer. When the fall sets and you bring them inside they will continue flowering until winter. Fuchsias look best when planted in hanging baskets, but can also look very good in mixed garden containers. They are especially beautiful when they are paired with contrasting colors plants; but complimentary color flowers would make a beautiful arrangement as well.

Their reputation for being fussy could be because they tend to wilt without the right amounts of fertilizer and water. Fuchsias need their soil moist at all times; not wet. They also will wilt when exposed to hot and dry conditions.

Wishbone Flower (*Torenia*) - the wishbone flower spreads cheer wherever it is planted for it will flower all through the summer especially when left in full shade. This flower tolerates heat well and is not fussy about anything.

To flower well, it requires regular fertilizing and watering until frost; you need not remove the dead flowers in order to have it flower well. You can use the Wishbone flower alone in its own container or in combinations with other flowers.

They are commonly used in hanging baskets, but they do well in window boxes also. Their only demand is that the container has good drainage. These flowers are relatively short in height - 2-6 inches - and will spill over the side of the container filling it up totally.

Coral Bells (*Heucheras*) - these are the best flowers you could ever have in containers in shade. They are so resilient that you could almost say they are indestructible and come in a wide range of colors. Coral bells love the shade, thought they will do well in some sun. They are quite drought tolerant and do not need to have the dead flowers removed to ensure continuous flowering.

Coral bells are very colorful; you will find them in colors that range from peach to limes to black-purple. Hummingbirds and butterflies and quite attracted to these flowers. To ensure that the plants continue to flower, you would do good to remove flower stems after they have bloomed.

Begonias (*Begonia*) - there are many varieties of begonias each one more beautiful than the other. They are bright, colorful and extremely resilient. Some begonias even have colorful leaves. What is most interesting about this plant is that they have some of the most amazing flowers and they will stay in bloom throughout the summer through late in the fall.

These flowers need good drainage or they will suffer from root rot. Most will be happy in full shade, while some varieties would need filtered shade. All flowering begonias require regular fertilizing and misting of the leaves and the soil.

Coleus (*Coleus blumei*) - Coleus are exceptionally well adapted for shade container gardening. They demand little attention; some will even thrive in full sun. The colors, leaves shapes, and even blooms are widely varied, interesting and exciting. Paired with other plants the coleus can look spectacular. You can have lots of fun with match- and-mixing this plant. No matter where you are putting it, they will steal the show.

[End of Excerpt] If you enjoyed reading this excerpt from *Container Gardening: How To Grow Food, Flowers and Fun at Home, you can grab your copy here:* http://amzn.to/RKWxmR

ABOUT THE AUTHOR

Will Cook is an avid gardener and loves growing his own fresh food on his balcony. Will believes the world would be a better place if everyone cared for a few plants and grew their own food (even if it's just a little bit).

Connect with Will on Facebook at http://on.fb.me/HmllNU

OTHER RECOMMENDED BOOKS ON GARDENING

<u>The Vertical Gardening Guidebook: How To Create Beautiful Vertical Gardens, Container Gardens and Aeroponic Vertical Tower Gardens at Home</u>

This is a great book for anyone interested in learning how to grow vertical gardens which allow you to grow more food in less space.

<u>Indoor Gardening: How To Grow Gorgeous Gardens Indoors With Ease</u>

This book is perfect for anyone who wants to grow an indoor garden for food, fun or just to create a gorgeous ambiance in your home. Did you know that some plants can remove as much as 87% of the toxins in your home in just 24 hours?

<u>Container Gardening: How To Grow Food, Flowers and Fun At Home</u>

This book is great if you want to create gorgeous, fun container gardens at home including detailed instructions for terrariums, growing succulents, bonsais and other fun and unique plants.

One Last Thing...

If you enjoyed this book or found it useful I'd be very grateful if you'd post a short review on Amazon. Your support really does make a difference and I read all the reviews personally so I can get your feedback and make this book even better.

If you'd like to leave a review then all you need to do is click the review link on this book's page on Amazon here: http://amzn.to/ZhGCjy

Thanks again for your support!

34375498R00064

Made in the USA
Lexington, KY
03 August 2014